Overview

This guide is meant to explain Donald Trump's personality and his likely actions as the President of the United States. It is written from the point of view of an FBI profile in order to predict actions and responses.

FBI profiling serves two purposes. It not only helps investigators determine the traits of an unknown assailant, it also serves **to predict behavior and reactions** to certain events, even after the assailant is known and in custody. A behavioral profile can be used during police questioning and even to set a courtroom strategy for the prosecution.

Since we already know the identity of the person we are profiling, we can more easily construct a profile and use it to determine Donald Trump's personality and his likely actions. This book should also enable you to predict actions and will serve to prevent you from being shocked and surprised over the next few years.

Please note that this profile does not come from the FBI, it is merely in the style of an FBI behavioral analysis. The author has researched FBI profiling techniques and has compiled the information into this thorough profile of Donald Trump in order to predict behavior. The author is not an FBI agent, consultant, and is not currently affiliated with the FBI in any way. Dr. Decker is merely a pen name.

Furthermore, this profile is not meant as a pro or anti Donald Trump message. It is meant as a neutral, clinical, and honest appraisal of the President's personality and a prediction of his likely actions.

Table of Contents

Section 1 – Introduction to FBI Profiling

The FBI formed their behavioral psychology unit in 1970 in order to study the minds of serial killers. The information obtained via this program gave investigators much more than the ability to define likely characteristics of a murderer-- it actually enabled investigators to **predict and manipulate** behavior and even the criminal's legal strategy.

We've all heard about a profiler's ability to determine that a killer would likely drive a green car and be between 25-30 years old. But this is not the ability we seek in this case. We seek the other advantage of profiling, namely the ability to **predict future behavior**.

The reason profiling can work is because people with a certain personality tend to do the same things from a long list of behaviors specific to that personality. So it is fair to say that people who do **some** of the things from that personality's list have a high chance of doing **other** things from that same list. That is how one can predict behavior or know that a person has likely engaged in certain behavior in the past.

Donald Trump's profile is included in the following chapter. If you wish to see two real-life examples of predicting behavior from FBI profiles, they are included below. The lessons here teach us that specific information and the tone of communication led to predictable action.

Example #1 The Atlanta Child Murderer

Young boys were being killed in Atlanta for two years beginning in 1979. Their bodies were being left in alleys and abandoned lots around the city. The FBI assisted with the investigation and formed a profile. One aspect of the profile was that the killer would closely follow the news of the investigation.

After one of the murders, a medical investigator said too much in an interview with a reporter and revealed that they were getting great evidence from the bodies. The FBI predicted that the killer would have seen this interview and would instead dump the bodies in rivers to hinder the collection of evidence. So they setup patrol cars to secretly watch every bridge of Atlanta's two major rivers all day and night. Sure enough, a large splash was heard late one night as a sole driver dumped something off a bridge. The driver was pulled over. His name was Wayne Bertram Williams. He was promptly investigated, arrested, and eventually found guilty of the Atlanta child murders.

In this case the ability to predict behavior led to a crucial arrest.

But predicting his behavior did not stop there. Williams had taken the stand during his trial and portrayed himself as calm and articulate for two entire days of questioning. It was clear that the jury was not sure he was capable of murder. The FBI profiler worked with the prosecuting attorney to determine how to upset Wayne Williams so that he would show anger. Using the profiler's specific advice for the third day on the stand, the prosecutor grabbed William's hands, invaded his space, and asked him a very specific question about how it felt to kill. Just as predicted by the profiler, Williams got extremely angry and had an outburst that showed the jury his dark side. He was later found guilty.

Example #2 The Beltway Sniper

In 2002, the inhabitants of the Washington DC area were living in terror. Someone or some people were randomly shooting and killing people from long distances as the victims left stores or put gas in their cars.

Charles Moose, the Montgomery County Chief of Police at the time, became the spokesman of the investigation. The FBI told him that the killer would have a god complex and to talk to him with respect and even fearfully, or else the killer(s) would prove to him that they are powerful. He was told that to minimize shootings, he should imply that the shooter has the power, and to use phrases like "this is in God's hands" to give the killer satisfaction and keep him calm. Moose did not listen to this advice and wanted to do it his own way. In a press conference, he told citizens not to be afraid, that everything was being done to catch the killer and that the streets and schools are safe. He even called the killer a coward. The next day, the sniper shot a child on his way to school and left a tarot card with a message "Dear Mr Policeman, call me God". Moose began to speak to the killers through the media in the way he was coached. This reduced the rate of shootings until the killers were eventually caught.

In this case, the tone of the communication and specific words resulted in predicted behavior and could have prevented certain behavior.

These are two examples where knowing the psychology of a total stranger enabled the prediction of their actions. Now we will examine Donald Trump to predict his behavior as President.

Section 2 – The Profile of Donald Trump

In his book Dangerous Personalities, author and former FBI agent David Navarro explains that there are four personality types that are responsible for much of the crime and difficulty on our planet. Thus there are four separate personality profiles for each that the FBI uses. These personality types are Narcissist, Predator, Emotionally Unstable, and Paranoid. Each has a scale, therefore some people may be more mild while others are extreme and actually dangerous. My first book teaches how to use FBI profiling on coworkers of these types in order to protect your job and your well being at work. For this book, we only need to focus on one of these types.

In honest and no uncertain terms, Donald Trump is the textbook example of a **narcissist** of the highest degree.

Thus we now turn our attention to the general profile of a narcissist in this section before proceeding to Donald Trump's future behavior.

Now what is a narcissist? Unfortunately, people confuse the definition with someone who simply cares too much about their appearance or likes looking at themselves in the mirror.

A narcissist is much more than that. They are essentially a psychopath who lacks any real empathy. The thought process of the narcissist can be summed up with these three thoughts:

- It's all about me
- Other people are "paper people" and do not matter
- The rules don't apply to me

It's All About Me

All children go through a phase where they think they are the center of the world and everything around them is for them, and they expect all people around them to cater to them and give them love and attention. And then they outgrow this phase.

The narcissist does not outgrow this phase. Part of their brains are stuck in the phase, yet the rest of their minds and body grow up. The narcissist is an adult with a fully developed mind and body with adult desires and abilities, but with the attention cravings and entitlement of a child.

Paper People

The narcissist does not care about other people or their feelings. They are missing the gene or neuro-net that causes empathy. <u>They are no different than psychopaths in personality</u>. In popular culture, the term psychopath usually refers to a murderer or someone that has committed a crime, but that is not always accurate.

A psychopath is the same thing as a narcissist, it is someone with no empathy for other people. But not all psychopaths/narcissists have committed crimes or hurt people. Most narcissists do not have the desire to physically hurt people or commit violent crimes. But those that do and commit crimes are often referred to "psychopathic murderers".

Thus there are millions of psychopaths/narcissists walking around that have not committed violent crimes, albeit they usually cause problems in other ways. Donald Trump is of this type, non-murderous.

This personality disorder affects millions of people. It works on a spectrum, or range. The more severe end of this spectrum is where criminals, murderers, cult leaders, and dictators reside. The middle of the spectrum is where the typical jerk and bully reside. The lower end is where self-centered attention cravers lay, even though they may be introverts.

The Rules Don't Apply to Me

Narcissists do not care about any rules, codes, or ethics. Those rules are for other people to follow, the lesser beings that need to be told what to do, the sheep. The narcissist feels they are entitled to do whatever they want. They are special. They are God's gift to the world.

They have no problem breaking codes of ethics, but they know enough not to get caught or be seen doing it. They do have a problem breaking laws since they are afraid of being caught. This is not out of some sense of right or wrong, but because they are afraid of suffering the fine, ticket, hassle, HR department, police, or jail.

These are the three underlying thoughts or the "operation system" of a narcissist. Now we will examine their profile. Below are the typical motivations, traits, and actions of a narcissist. Those who commit a few of these actions are likely to commit others. This is how we will predict Donald Trump's presidency in Section 3.

Motivation

In one sentence: The narcissist wants power and attention.

These things are more important than money to the narcissist. They expect other people to be constantly in awe of them, give them attention, and cater to their wishes. They want to dominate and have influence. Money is just a nice way of showing their success or leveraging power, but power is what they crave most.

They will do anything to take power and control. While they know enough not to break laws, they have no problem breaking ethics or any societal/corporate code of conduct. There is a huge difference between illegal and unethical. Most people follow both a code of law and ethics, such as not lying or manipulating. Narcissists know enough to follow the law only to avoid jail and police. However, narcissists have no ethics. They know that it is not illegal to lie or manipulate. They rely on other people to follow ethics so that they can be played like chess pieces or used like tools.

They are attracted to positions of power such as business executive, lawyer, politician, or police officer. In fact, one study suggests that CEOs are four times more likely to be a psychopath. Usually one out of one hundred people is a psychopath, but for CEOs it is four out of one hundred. Obviously not all or even most members of these professions are narcissists, but know that they can gravitate towards these positions.

It is best not to focus on why they are this way. This guide is meant to deal with the "what" without digging into volumes of psychological studies, articles, or analysis. Now you will learn about how they operate and we can apply this to Donald Trump to predict his actions as president.

Below are the common words that describe and the common actions of narcissists. This is the key to predicting behavior. Remember that profiling works by identifying someone's personality and then noting their past and likely future actions from this list. There are different lists for different personality types, but we are only concerned with the Narcissist's traits and actions for the profile of Donald Trump.

Note that these lists were written years ago about narcissists in general and not specifically for Donald Trump. You can decide which of these traits and actions apply to Donald Trump.

Narcissist Descriptions/Traits

- Heavily attracted to power, grandiose
- Ass Kisser
- Name Dropper

- Nosey
- Information Hoarder
- Sneaky, conniving, schemer, manipulative
- Thinks he/she is flawless and great at everything
- Entitled, privileged
- Superficially charming, charismatic, clever, interesting
- Controlling
- Cold, callous, insincere, inconsiderate, affectionless, emotionless
- Chameleon, Two-faced
- Half assed, dilettante, dabbler, does not follow through
- Pushy, bully, belittler
- Slick talker, salesman, con-man, articulate,
- Liar, bluffer, bullshitter
- Motor mouth, overly talkative
- Sarcastic, witty
- Attention craver, domineering, egocentric

Common Actions

- Wants a hand in everything, always wants control
- Collects and hoards information
- Tries to take over or insert themselves into other people's work/projects
- Wants attention, hates when others get it and steers attention back to him/her, "one-ups" people
- Requires excessive admiration and loyalty
- Expects priority and special treatment

- May pay great attention to their own personal appearance and physique
- Must have the best of everything, high status brands
- Lies or exaggerates
- Inflates personal accomplishments, overvalues self and skill at most things
- Passes work onto others, doesn't finish what he/she starts but wants to take credit for it
- Claims others' work is lacking something and therefore he/she should be involved
- Manipulates people or situations to his/her advantage, exploits others for personal gain
- Insults others with name calling or childish logic
- Talks about need to lead, exercise power, or have immediate success
- Ignores other people's problems, suffering, and boundaries such as privacy
- When arguing, goes into wordy, illogical tangents unrelated to the discussion
- Shows up late to meetings for attention or makes big/theatrical entrances
- Takes shortcuts, bends rules, violates boundaries
- Often drops names of higher ups at their workplace or even celebrities with which he/she has interacted
- Mainly wants to associate with other special, powerful, or high status people

- Skilled at finding and pointing out other people's weaknesses. Calls attention to others weaknesses, mistakes, or social faux pas
- Often puts others down in attempts to bond with others or appear funny
- Overvalues self, devalues others and puts other people down, bullies or cyber bullies others
- Devalues co-workers to the manager
- When losing, is quick to say the situation or world is unfair
- Uses attentiveness, catering to, and gifts to get things from others or win people over
- Uses friendships as a function, to receive something wanted or needed
- Jumps from friendship to friendship or relationship
- Asks personal or invasive questions as if they are asking what you had for lunch
- Asks many questions in a row to control the conversation and make you feel like you are answering to them
- Conversations are mainly one-way, talking at you and not with you
- Holds grudges and aims to bring others down who get in their way
- Envies others or believes others are envious of him/her
- May try to convince you that someone is your enemy or that you need to take action against someone

- Intentionally does not validate something you have accomplished
- Assumes others value him/her highly and are surprised if they learn they do not
- Possibly lied or greatly exaggerated something on his/her resume, claimed to be something they are not
- Gets extremely angry when ability or methods are questioned
- Attempts to put the blame on you if you claim they did something wrong to you

Tactics and Ways of Working

They have become masters at telling people what they want or need to hear.

They have superficial knowledge about many things which they use to appear intelligent and well versed. They will remember the occasional interesting fact or quotation in order to sound intellectual. They express themselves with great conviction in order to sound like their opinions are facts or their misinformation are facts. They are conversational chameleons. They often have the ability to blend in with many different types of people and personalities. They excel at working people, not actual work. They often do not follow through on things they say they will do. They are classic namedroppers, mentioning a higher up at the office they have spoken with, or perhaps a celebrity. They exaggerate, bluff, and downright lie.

They are information hoarders. They want to know what everyone is doing while not sharing information that only they know. They love the idea of knowing something that no one else knows, it is a very strong feeling of power to them. They may even initialize work or new methods without telling anyone first or asking permission.

They want to be involved in all projects for the purposes of getting credit, seeming important & involved, and for information collecting. Their involvement will be superficial and they will make little if any actual contribution. They often make false or empty promises on what they will eventually contribute or pay back.

They will use any tactic, no matter how underhanded, to get what they want. If it is not illegal, no matter how low it is deemed by society, they will do it.

They hate when other people receive praise around them. They will try to draw the attention back to themselves. They can even show up late for meetings just for attention, so they can hear "Now we can start."

They repeatedly enter and lose friendships. They come across as charming at first, but after time people realize how selfish and uncaring they are. So they go from friendship to friendship and tend not to have a lifelong best friend. Those that remain friends with narcissists tend to have low self esteem and are attracted to the narcissist's confidence, hoping it will somehow "rub off" on them. But it never does as confidence must come from within. A narcissist in a relationship or friendship will occasionally pretend to care because they recognize it as a way to fit in or get something in return. They do not care who they step on or offend to get what they want. They almost never say "I'm sorry". The only self analyzing they do is to see how they can be better at what they're trying to attain.

Since they cannot answer questions correctly and thoroughly with only superficial knowledge, they will give "word salad" answers that go off in tangents, but yet sound important and factual. If in a disagreement, they try to bulldoze someone with unrelated information but they say it emphatically in order to show no doubt and absolute authority over the subject-matter. They may give a list of points or information that do not logically or factually tie to any point.

To make a narcissist angry, simply question their ability or judgment. How dare a "paper person" question them. They will raise their voice and may even get physical. They usually make false threats and will try to appear to have more ability than they do. They will make a false threat to sue, tell your boss, or "ruin you". But they do not have that ability and it is only an empty threat. If they had the power to get other people out of their way, they would have used it long ago. They are false threats intended to get you to back down, give in, give them what they want, or to prevent you from telling HR or someone about them. They also say those things to feel powerful and to keep up the illusion that they are in control, have power, and should be feared or respected.

This person will lie, cheat, and steal to get ahead. "Steal" in this sense means to take underhandedly and not necessarily illegally. They will try to collect information on everything and everyone, as well as try to have their hand in everything. At work, their primary method is to attain projects and people in order for their importance, title, and power to grow. They will often ask to takeover projects and even personnel to manage.

Now that you know a narcissist's motivation, description, and common actions, let us use this profile to predict the presidency of Donald Trump. Note that you could easily compare Donald Trump's past actions and statements to the items on this list to confirm the diagnosis for yourself. You should also note that all of this may sound like an anti-Trump message, but it is intended to be clinical, non-partisan, and unemotional. He is simply a narcissist and this fact will greatly affect his actions as president, actions that I attempt to predict in the next chapter. So no matter if you are "for" or "against" Donald Trump, you will not be surprised by the next four years.

Section 3 – What to Expect from the Trump Presidency

For the record, the day of this writing is January 19, 2017. Donald Trump's inauguration is tomorrow. This book will be completed and published on Amazon by Monday January 23rd, thus you can easily determine if these predictions have come true if you are reading this in the months/years that follow. Also, the more you read the profile of a narcissist in the previous section, the more you will be able to predict on your own.

The following section describes predictions of Donald Trump's administration, domestic, foreign, and economic initiatives.

Donald Trump will do the following things as President:

Appoint people based on personal connections and superficial charm instead of based on their qualifications. He will likely appoint other narcissists or total sycophants. He will not thoroughly vet/screen his selections. He will continue to appoint family members and other friends and relatives to high profile positions even though they are not experienced. This will result in a cabinet of people acting for their own interest and image, based on personal whims. His cabinet will not have any unified action, message, nor consistency. Many random initiatives will be taken. Lobbyists and corporations will closely monitor and exploit this situation. They will develop personal relationships with cabinet members and exploit the lack of thorough leadership and unified goals for corporate interest and quid pro quo relationships. Thus Trump's appointees for the various departments of government will be acting in their own interests with no supervision. Their only restraint will be the public finding out about their actions. At first they will change very little with their own initiatives, however, they will eventually begin launching programs created by corporations, lobbyists, and the people who have access to them.

Many attempts will be made for the privatization of many aspects of life, including schools and especially prisons. This will become a huge talking point by the media and the American public.

In general, President Trump will be manipulated by flattery in exchange for favors and directives.

He will tax US corporations for sending jobs to other countries Keeping jobs in the US will be the major focus of his presidency, as well as removing any economic trade advantage given to foreign countries.

He will seek to stimulate manufacturing in the United States and will especially push automakers to increase manufacturing within the US.

He will fully attempt to build the wall and fence along the US/Mexican border.

He will work on initiatives that mean something to him emotionally – US jobs, immigration, and security.

He will increase spending on border patrol and enforcement. Millions of people are typically deported while trying to enter the US over a 4-8 year period. Approximately 2.5 million people were deported during the Obama administration as part of normal border patrol and immigration policy. Naturally, a similar number will be deported during Donald Trump's presidency. Trump will take credit for these deportations even though they are not related to him or any of his initiatives. He will do little to change immigration policy, but will create an initiative to deport illegal immigrants with criminal records. He will boast about that immigration number as his popularity slides.

He and congress will not successfully repeal the Affordable Care Act (Obamacare) without an adequate substitute. He will instead seek to remove certain aspects of it. The specifics of it will take three years to be worked out. It will be a frustrating time period for the American public who use or consider using it for medical coverage.

He will not spend money unnecessarily and will likely reduce government spending. Some government jobs will be lost due to these cutbacks. Trump will claim that more jobs will be created in the private sector as a result and that balanced spending is better for the government and the people. Specifically, he will seek to cut many social programs, especially those that seem like "handouts". He will seek to cut or restrict programs like welfare, saying that aid should only go to those looking for or willing to work. Conversely, he is likely to extend unemployment benefits to those looking for work for longer than 26 weeks.

He will reduce spending and resources for intelligence agencies.

He will do very little to support the public school system and teachers. He will recommend that more people turn to private schools.

He will do nothing to increase gun control.

When a national or local tragedy strikes, especially a mass shooting or ISIS –inspired terrorist attack, his speeches will not be about tolerance and love, but about anger and revenge.

With regard to personal comments and decorum—he will likely offend multiple women at nighttime galas and parties when he feels he is "off the clock". He will continue to make sexual comments and innuendos both on and off camera. He may specifically mention or attempt to brag/exaggerate about his genitalia size. He will focus his photo-opts on visiting corporations and manufacturing facilities instead of school children, the poor, and the military. He will not be very friendly to children and may even make one cry during a photo-op or school visit. When interacting with military personnel, at first he will not be respectful enough when meeting soldiers and members of the military. He will likely offend military families and supporters with an off the cuff remark. This will not be as severe as he did with Mr. and Mrs. Kahn, but at first he will take some criticism for not being respectful enough. Over time, he will see how important respecting the military is for a President's approval and he will begin to show more respect and photo-ops.

He will continue to clash with reporters and the press. More and more journalists, even popular network journalists, will boldly condemn and speak out against Trump as his popularity decreases.

He will secretly devote time each day to receive status reports for his own business and financial interests, despite the business being managed by his children and the conflict of interest.

Will likely use Air Force One to visit his own golf courses, hotels, resorts, and projects to check on things, or he will plan official visits to areas near them so that he can visit his properties. He will travel by helicopter more than other presidents in the past in order to view his properties from a closer vantage point.

He will occasionally move the stock market up and down with careless statements and Tweets.

He will increase spending for police, SWAT teams, and aggressive anti-gang task forces. This will result in some arrests but no sweeping changes to gun violence.

He will personally monitor Twitter and the media to see what different people are saying about him. He will constantly monitor his approval rating at first. Over time, his approval rating will likely slip as he does not follow through on some of his campaign promises. He will retreat into spending more time with his staunch supporters and inner-circle. Privately, he will bounce between cycles of closely monitoring his approval rating and totally ignoring it. If he is ever asked about his low approval rating, he will publicly claim that he does not know what his approval rating is, or that the rating is flawed or somehow biased against him. His mood will shift between wanting to be liked by liberals on the "other side" to anger and resentment at them, resulting in occasionally offending liberals and small exertions of power and neglect as a reminder.

During public appearances and speeches, he will bounce between remaining totally "on script" from his speech writers when he feels tired or lazy to "winging it" when he feels he is not in control or if the message does not match his public image.

Some will call for impeachment for various reasons, but a lack of decorum is not enough for an impeachment. While there is currently talk about impeachment for possible collusion by Trump with Russia for election hacking, no evidence will be found.

Trump will have many staff changes at the lower levels. Those not being paid enough to deal with his changing behavior and empty promises will quit. The excitement of working for a president will not be enough to keep lower level workers from quitting when they are unhappy.

When he feels the need for an ego boost, he will make many public speeches similar to his campaign rallies in order receive adulation from crowds in person.

He will not take any action to affect climate change policy. He will leave that up to congress and the EPA and will not spend much time addressing that issue. He may pull the United States out of the Paris climate deal.

He will try to score points with women by discussing the perceived wage inequality and harsher punishments for sex offenders. While he appears sexist, his sexism is not general to all women. He sees some women as sex objects that he does not respect and can say whatever he wants to. However, he sees other women differently. If he does not see a specific woman as a sex object, he can actually respect her mind. Thus he will appoint some women to higher positions. Yet, he tends to gravitate towards blond hair and blue eyed women either way.

More accusations from women will surface from when Trump was in his 20s and 30s.

He will try to appoint an extremely conservative and relatively young justice to the Supreme Court as the first step in eventually reversing Roe vs Wade in the distant future.

With regard to foreign affairs, he will distance the United States from NATO in participation, the UN Security Council, and international military support.

He will not help foreign countries in need of economic or military aid unless manipulated into it by advisors, cabinet, military industrial complex, or generals. He will also greatly reduce foreign aid. This will result in increased tensions and an unfavorable view from many countries around the world.

He will be tested by foreign countries via cyber-attacks and attempted terrorist attacks. Cuts to the intelligence agencies will increase the risk of both types of attacks.

He would use military action if he feels he is being perceived as "weak", is dared into it, or his approval rating is low. He is more likely to use military action on an offensive small nation that cannot strike back, such as North Korea (see below).

Tensions with China will increase, especially economically. Trump has already said that he does not like the currency fixing employed by China and that the US is already "too nice" to them. Trump will consider increasing duty costs for US companies manufacturing products in China.

With regard to Iran, he will not follow through on the negotiation made by the Obama administration and will not support any payments to Iran. This will result in increased tensions with Iran.

Russia will continue to act in its own interest regarding the Ukraine, Crimea, and the Black and Caspian Seas. Trump will do little to resist Russian advances. Putin will see that the best way to perform aggressive acts will be to do them infrequently, or little by little. Thus Trump will not be forced to respond to any one large aggressive act, but instead can ignore or down play infrequent smaller moves, which he will do.

North Korea will likely become the new conflict. Increased tension with North Korea seems very likely, especially if Kim Jong-un makes any publicly threatening or disparaging remarks against the United States or Donald Trump himself. If Donald Trump feels he is being challenged or is perceived as "weak" by the United States media or public around the time of inflammatory North Korea action or talk, Trump would likely want to respond with military action. Trump would have no issue attacking a small country like North Korea, especially with a leader who he feels should not dare to talk tough. Trump would likely use an unexpected long range missile and drone strikes to send a message. His advisors and generals would likely push for a large strike to cripple North Korea's long range missile capabilities in the first strike. This will result in North Korea attacking civilian ships and naval battles, and increased tensions with China. China would be facing a mass immigration problem in the event of a conflict in North Korea. The conflict will not result in all out war, but Trump's military action will be deemed unnecessary by US citizens, especially without a build up by the US media.

In general, any military action will be taken with missiles, jets, bombers, and drones, as Trump will not want to get his "hands dirty" by using troops. He will strike from a distance and above, as someone with a God complex would.

Trump will reduce spending on the war on drugs in other countries, such as bombing/destroying crops in other countries. He will focus more on border patrol and security around ports and the US/Mexico border.

He will continue to insult and disrespect Muslims and will not cooperate with countries whose major religion is Islam.

He will do little to help or maintain relations with Native Americans.

With regard to the economy:

He will clash with the Federal Reserve often and will try attain and exercise control and influence over them. Note that despite the name, the Federal Reserve is a privately owned bank and a separate entity from the United States Government. His clashes with the Fed will result in the occasional volatile stock market day.

A slight recession will begin between 2017-2021. It will start as a stock market correction as interest rates rise and the money supply tightens without quantitative easing. As stock prices and buying decrease, the banking/financial sector will be hit first, followed by consumer confidence, the retail sector, real estate, and corporate hiring and salaries. Layoffs will begin and unemployment will rise. Trump will not want to cooperate with the Federal Reserve to resolve the issue. He will be surprised when his cost cutting measures on foreign aid and keeping jobs here are not enough to support the number of new jobs needed every month to keep unemployment even. He will not do enough to slow the recession and this will be large issue in the 2020 election that will sway voters. He will likely lose the 2020 election as the economy shows signs of a recession and what was perceived as unnecessary military action.

Conclusion

Donald Trump's presidency will be an extension of his personality. As a narcissist, he will only work on a superficial level and plan on hiring minions to handle details. Since he is not dealing with his business and his own money, he will not vet personnel as thoroughly as he would. The people he chooses will be a combination of other narcissists and well connected yes-men. There will be no clear voice or unity from his administration, cabinet, and white house. His main focus will be manufacturing jobs, trade, government spending, and border security. Anything beyond these issues will receive little attention from Trump and will be left to the discretion of whomever he has appointed to head the relevant department.

There will continue to be conflict of interest violations that he ignores, as well as decorum issues with Twitter, women, and military personnel and families.

As a show of strength and an approval rating boost, you can expect a cruise missile, drone, or B-17 attack ordered by Trump on a small offensive country, specifically North Korea or similar.

Foreign relations will be at an all time low. US tensions will rise with China and Iran. Russia will pursue its own agenda gradually and unchecked.

He will have success in reducing government spending to foreign countries, but this will not solve the federal deficit.

As the economy declines with rising interest rates, Trump will not work with the Federal Reserve to create the proper policy. This will result in the beginning of a recession. He will have some success with keeping jobs in the United States, but they will not be enough to create 145,000 jobs per month to keep the employment rate the same. In addition, jobs lost from government cuts at home will stick with him as a negative point.

The total job loss, stock declines, and lack of proper action to curb the recession will cause Trump to lose the 2020 election, as well as unnecessary military action.

Made in the USA
Middletown, DE
05 July 2020